Living and Nonliving in the Desert

Rebecca Rissman

Heinemann
LIBRARY

Chicago, Illinois

© 2014 Heinemann Library
an imprint of Capstone Global Library, LLC
Chicago, Illinois

To contact Capstone Global Library please phone
800-747-4992, or visit our website
www.capstonepub.com

Edited by Daniel Nunn, Rebecca Rissman, and
Catherine Veitch
Designed by Cynthia Della-Rovere
Picture research by Tracy Cummins
Production by Sophia Argyris
Originated by Capstone Global Library Ltd

ISBN 978-1-4109-5380-3 (hc)
ISBN 978-1-4109-5387-2 (pb)

Library of Congress Cataloging-in-Publication Data

Rissman, Rebecca.
  Living and nonliving in the desert / Rebecca Rissman.
     pages cm.—(Is it living or nonliving?)
  Includes bibliographical references and index.
  ISBN 978-1-4109-5380-3 (hb)—ISBN 978-1-4109-5387-
2 (pb) 1. Deserts—Juvenile literature. 2. Life (Biology)—
Juvenile literature. I. Title.

  QH88.R567 2013
  577.54—dc23   2012046869

Printed and bound in the USA.
009956RP

Acknowledgments

We would like to thank the following for permission to
reproduce photographs: Alamy p. 12 (© Bill Gozansky);
istockphoto pp. 1 (© Erik Bettini), 21 (© Paul Erickson);
Shutterstock pp. 4, 23a (© Junker), 5 (© SNEHIT), 6, 23b
(© hagit berkovich), 7 (© EcoPrint), 8 (© Jan Kratochvila),
9 (© Igor Janicek), 10, 23c (© orxy), 11 (© Worachat
Sodsri), 13 (© urosr), 14, 23d (© Galyna Andrushko),
15 (© LouLouPhotos), 16 (© Vladimir Wrangel), 17
(© taelove7), 18 (© Patrick Poendl), 19 (© Fatseyeva),
22 (© Anton Prado PHOTO); Superstock p. 20 (© Minden
Pictures).

Front cover photograph of a thorny devil, crossing cracked
mud in Australia reproduced with permission of Getty
Images (© Minden Pictures).

We would like to thank Michael Bright and Nancy Harris for
their invaluable help in the preparation of this book.

Some words are in bold, **like this**.
You can find them in the glossary on page 23.

Contents

What Is a Desert?

A desert is a dry **habitat**.

Many deserts are very hot during the day and cold at night.

Different types of plants and animals live in the desert.

There are **nonliving** things in the desert too.

What Are Living Things?

Living things are alive. Living things need air and **sunlight**. Living things need food and water.

Living things grow and change.

Living things move on their own.

What Are Nonliving Things?

Nonliving things are not alive. Nonliving things do not need air and **sunlight**.

Nonliving things do not need food or water.

Nonliving things do not grow and change on their own.

Nonliving things do not move on their own.

Is a Rock Living or Nonliving?

A rock does not need food or water.

A rock does not need air and **sunlight**.

A rock does not move on its own.

A rock does not grow or change on its own.

A rock is **nonliving**.

Is a Lizard Living or Nonliving?

A lizard needs food and water.

A lizard moves on its own.

A lizard grows and changes.

A lizard needs air and **sunlight**.

A lizard is **living**.

Is a Cactus Living or Nonliving?

A cactus grows and changes.

A cactus moves on its own toward the sun.

A cactus needs water.

A cactus needs air and **sunlight**.

A cactus is **living**.

Is Sand Living or Nonliving?

Sand does not move on its own.

Sand does not grow and change on its own.

Sand does not need food or water.

Sand does not need air and **sunlight**.

Sand is **nonliving**.

Is a Camel Living or Nonliving?

A camel grows and changes.

A camel moves on its own.

A camel needs food and water.

A camel needs air and **sunlight**.

A camel is **living**.

Is a Spider Living or Nonliving?

A spider moves on its own.

A spider needs food and water.

A spider grows and changes.

A spider needs air and **sunlight**.

A spider is **living**.

What Do You Think?

Is this soil **living** or **nonliving**?

Glossary

habitat place where plants and animals live

living alive. Living things need food and water. They breathe and move on their own. They grow and change.

nonliving not alive. Nonliving things do not need food and water. They do not move on their own. They do not grow and change on their own.

sunlight light from the sun

Find Out More

Websites

Facthound offers a safe, fun way to find Internet sites related to this book. All of the sites on Facthound have been researched by our staff.

Here's all you do:
Visit www.facthound.com
Type in this code: 9781410953803

Books

Ganeri, Anita. *Harsh Habitats (Extreme Nature)*. Chicago: Raintree, 2013.

Slade, Suzanne. *What Eats in a Desert Food Chain (Food Chains)*. Mankato, Minn.: Capstone, 2013.

Waldron, Melanie. *Deserts (Habitat Survival)*. Chicago: Raintree, 2013.

Index